Healing from toxic family:

Steps on handling toxic family members.

1

Table of contents

Chapter 1

Chapter 2

Chapter 3

Chapter 4

Chapter 5

Chapter 1

Toxicity

Toxic behavior definition refers to a person whose behavior and continuing acts cause harm to other individuals through physical or mental ways. These are the persons that propagate bad or poisonous stress or traumas on others. Toxic behavior is not regarded as a mental condition but is produced by a mental problem which is largely expressed in personality disorders and odd qualities in human behavior.

At some time in our life, we all come across someone that creates a lot of troubles in our lives. They may stir up difficulties and be the reason for certain disagreements. These folks are genuinely poisonous persons, based on the characteristics they display.

The toxic features of a toxic person include unsupportive and unpleasant conduct, being manipulative, judgemental, dominating, and self-centered. Such people might be the cause of different unpleasant sentiments and emotions that you may be experiencing including sadness, nervousness, worthlessness, and dissatisfaction.

Most often than not, a toxic person might be your closest friend, someone you have known all your life, or someone who came into your life abruptly like a colleague or college acquaintance and was suddenly extremely important to you. We tend to have blind spots for such people and we typically disregard their poisonous behavior regardless of how horrible and uncomfortable they often make us feel. In this post, we'll speak about how you may spot the poisonous behavior patterns shown by someone you are close to and what you can do to cope with such a person.

What is a Toxic Personality Disorder?
To put it in the most simple way, a toxic person is somebody whose behavior brings negativity and stress to your life. We often find ourselves asking this question: "Why is this individual behaving this way?" And "what exactly drove this individual to be so toxic?" And there is typically an answer to these queries. Many people that behave in a toxic manner have been through trauma themselves, and instead of coping with that pain, these people start showing poisonous tendencies. These people frequently don't know how to handle trauma and stress in a

healthy manner, so they wind up being disagreeable around people.

Toxicity is not considered a mental condition however several mental problems can be the underlying cause of toxic conduct, such borderline personality disorder, post-traumatic stress disorder, or bipolar disorder. As Christian Baloga, an award-winning artist and novelist has said:

" Pay no heed to harmful remarks. What others say is frequently a reflection of themselves, not you.

Sign of a toxic family member

Some lucky people are born into families they like spending time with—their loving mutual relationships make holidays and multi-generational vacations a drama-free delight. But for others, merely seeing an incoming call from a parent sparks an anxiety that stretches back to childhood, and they leave family gatherings feeling wounded, angry, or fatigued. Toxic familial relationships can have a far-reaching influence on our lives as adults.

And narcissistic parenting isn't the only sort of poisonous family interaction. Fern Schumer Chapman, author of Brothers, Sisters, Strangers: Sibling Estrangement and the Road to Reconciliation, believes that this issue isn't nearly as talked about. "There's this assumption that siblings would have sustainable ties for all of their lives," she adds. "So when you respond that you don't, there's this concern of, 'is there anything wrong with you?'"

The truth might be far more convoluted. a toxic person is the result of a toxic environment themselves—so they frequently aren't even conscious of their own damaging tendencies. "I frequently joke that if you have one toxic person in your family, you definitely have ten," she adds. "Because that's what was modeled." Without assistance, it can be perpetuated further by marrying into other people's dysfunctional families.
Is someone who you're ideally intended to be close to actually motivating an impulse to defend yourself? Here are some indicators of a toxic family member, and professional advice on coping with a toxic

        9

family—because "drink all of the wine" is not a sustainable approach.

They make mercilessly scathing remarks. No one's known you longer than your family has, which means they've got a rich back history of personal failings to pull from when commenting on your life. Their frank critique might wound like a physical strike.

"Toxic parents demonstrate a chronic lack of empathy towards their children," trauma These behaviors might materialize through caustic remarks on looks, marital status, mental or physical health, financial issues, or work obstacles."

Even if they say they're simply joking, those statements may (even unconsciously) be decimating by purpose. "It's hard to envision a parent purposely taking cheap jabs at their children, but it occurs when

They give you the quiet treatment.
Yes, words may hurt—but so can their absence. If they refuse to talk to you for hours (or even days) following a dispute, it's a type of manipulation. This is true regardless of the family member.

"Toxic family members are known for utilizing silence as a method of punishment and emotional control," "They find power in being chased for a relationship."

They lie—or deny.
Even when it's a deception that doesn't include or affect you directly, lack of clarity about the truth produces uncertainty and cultivates a suspicion that leaves you wondering what else isn't true—particularly when it happens again. "They may even hide a lie with another lie," Denial may also take the shape of (patently incorrect) broad claims like, "we don't have secrets in this house."

They generalize during debates.
"Specific may be contested, but general charges are a lot tougher to dispute," The statements can sound something like, "it never works out," or "you always do this."

They foment tension with other family members.
Maybe they flat-out ask you why you can't be more like the sibling you've always felt competitive with, or they laud his triumphs in ways that underscore where you fall short. Or, they could relay something another family member said about you. "Unhealthy parents will put their children against one another, or against other members of the family," "They create settings where jealousy and hatred might develop."

They shift the subject to turn the tables on you.
In an argument, they could redirect attention by bringing up one of your

weaknesses, instead. For example: You tell a loved one you're concerned about their drug misuse, and they react with irrelevant charges that you're a horrible parent. They make you feel awful about feeling bad. It may be quite unpleasant when you're attempting to communicate your sadness over a grievance—or even abuse, committed by them or another family member—only to be left feeling like you injured them by bringing it up. They may cry or strike out with righteous rage. Or, they may remark something like, "Why can't you let things go?," thus discounting your bad experiences.

They move the goalposts. "Manipulative personalities typically modify the standards that people have to achieve in order to satisfy them," adds Chapman. "It's incredibly unpleasant, because just when you think you've done what they wanted, it's not good enough."

     13

They employ threats, harsh words, or violence.
This may seem like the most apparent symptom of a toxic relationship, but not if it's always been accepted as part of your family dynamic. There's never any scenario in which name-calling or physical intimidation and other types of domestic abuse are justifiable, and if you fear for your safety, help is available.

They're a maestro of passive-aggressive conduct.
This might involve guilt trips and backhanded compliments,coupled with nonverbal signals such as rolling eyes and sighs.
They make your business your great-aunt Lydia's business.
A blooming romance suddenly ended, and though you had no need to be humiliated, you didn't want the whole world to know about your love sadness. Enter your mother, who's shared your narrative as a means to

relate (or worse, share a laugh) with someone else.

It's not unusual for a toxic family member to break your confidence. "They'll often reveal personal information or life issues with anybody they think worthy of knowing, with little-to-no concern for how these breaches of trust damage their children's emotional well-being."

They gaslight you.

A phrase inspired by the 1944 Ingrid Bergman film Gaslight, gaslighting is a sort of emotional abuse in which someone convinces the victim to mistrust their own perception of reality. "They deny that the abuse is truly happening," adds Chapman. "It's confused and overwhelming, because all the sudden you're wondering that what you see and feel is real."(You can learn more about this aspect on my other book GASLIGHT AS AN ABUSE)

Examples she cites include a sibling stating your childhood experiences weren't as horrible as you recall, or a family member point-blank saying something like, "that didn't happen—you're making things up, as usual."

They ignore limits.
Setting appropriate boundaries is vital in good relationships; they can range from "please don't call me at work" to asking other family members to observe the limits that you set for your kids. If your preferences aren't being honored by someone who doesn't think the limits apply to them, it might make you feel like you're not being respected.

They play the blame game.
A parent, sibling, or other family member may often shift responsibility for everything that's wrong on someone else—possibly you, included. While their acts or conduct may not be the primary explanation for a specific situation, repeatedly refusing to accept any blame is a warning sign

A poisonous sibling may "side with" your parents.
In a well-adjusted family dynamic, there's typically no such thing as "picking sides."
But when someone learns negative relationship patterns from a parent, they may try to earn that parent's respect by imitating those patterns and thereby normalizing destructive conduct.

"Destructive siblings typically become a supporter of an equally toxic parent,"
"They'll use identical critical language as the parent, and embarrass the targeted sibling in areas of life they might be feeling sensitive about."

Fostering or participating in a competitive dynamic that's aimed to make you feel awful is another sort of toxic sibling conduct, as is casually forgetting your invite to family get-togethers. "Their intention is to deliver the unmistakable impression that you're not invited on purpose, and they'll frequently boast about what a magnificent occasion it is.

Beware of repeating destructive patterns with others.
You didn't pick the household you were raised in, but you can make sure you don't welcome new toxic influences into your life by presuming the awful ways they treat you are okay. "If one or both parents who raised you had considerably problematic qualities, your ability to identify red flags in the individuals you encounter will be badly harmed,Without actual awareness on how our home environment developed relationship blind spots, we face a significant danger of repeating destructive habits from infancy,These might include people-pleasing habits, difficulties regulating your temper, or being emotionally unavailable in adult relationships." Auditing your relationships' health via self-examination and the support

of a mental health expert can help you avoid reproducing the toxicity.

Before telling a toxic family member how they make you feel, try this.
If you don't believe that their conduct is serious enough to warrant cutting off contact—or you're simply not ready to take that dramatic step—you may be tempted to call them out, in an effort to stop the loop.
Just be cautious to temper your expectations of the conversation: Definitely don't think you'll get an explicit apology, or a rapid improvement in your dynamic. In fact, they may finish up pressing your buttons more than ever

The poisonous people will frequently seek to bring a heightened degree of emotions to the dialogue.On the opposite side of the spectrum, they can refuse to consider your problems." To assist keep your argument even-keeled and on topic, developing a list

of the person's most painful offenses and sticking to your talking points.
Detachment is key,
You have no influence over someone else's actions, but you can work on your own reaction to it. When going no-touch isn't an option that you're ready or able to pick.

"Detached touch concentrates on our capacity to be physically there, but not emotionally injured by the behavior of a family member.We fully identify the psychological tricks they're playing to draw a reaction.
Deciding to implement a no-contact rule is a huge move that may test your commitment, call for new family holiday customs, and push other family members to try and interfere. It's obviously not the single choice for every tumultuous family relationship nor is it the ideal solution for everyone. It also doesn't necessarily have to be permanent..

many situations need it—especially when earlier attempts to mend ties are futile. No-contact becomes an option to explore if the circumstance is seriously harming your mental health. "An rise in symptoms of sadness, anxiety, panic disorder, addictions, and emotional instability are all signals of essential distancing from a toxic family member,
It's an immensely terrible experience to confront the necessity of cutting a family member out of our life.It's a metaphorical death with complex grieving, because the family member is still breathing but emotionally dangerous."

Another reason adults may opt to protect themselves with a no-contact rule is out of worry that their own children would be exposed to the same inappropriate behaviors or blatant abuse. Poisonous parents usually become toxic grandparents.

Chapter 3

How it affect you

When it comes to letting go of connections with our toxic family members, we have certain alternatives accessible to us. I know from experience and through treating others that it is vital to attempt all of these possibilities. When we try everything, it makes our final decision to go no-contact more comfortable as we come to recognize the toxic individuals in our lives leaving us with no other alternative.
It's difficult for a youngster who grew up in a dysfunctional family dynamic to create good boundaries, have healthy self-esteem, and build respectful and loving relationships. Furthermore, they often replicate the parenting pattern they learnt in

their childhood and indulge in
self-destructive behavior as a form of
escape.

The sorrows of abuse resonate across
decades and can affect a person for life.
Were you the victim of any abuse or neglect
growing up? If yes, these are some of the
lifetime repercussions you've possibly
encountered.

1. Trust concerns
This is one of the most essential topics.
When children can't trust the parents who
gave them life, they grow up feeling that
they can't trust anyone.

2. Inability to put limits on abuse
They learn to forgive or dismiss poor
behavior. After all, they've grown up
witnessing their parents, caretakers, and

family members condone abusive conduct. Consequently, they're also expected to explain and minimize inappropriate behavior.

3. Learning not to talk about issues and waiting for them to burst
Members of a dysfunctional household learn to sweep problems under the rug. Communication skills are inadequate because no one wants to deal with difficulties, thus they spend little time interacting.

4. Anxiety and depression problems
Growing up in chaotic or uncertain surroundings influences how children manage stress. In fact, they're always on alert since they never know what'll come next.

Even after they're grown up and have a house of their own, their brain has been taught to live in a state of perpetual attention. This means their fight or flight mode doesn't become engaged as soon as that of others, as their body is habituated to greater amounts of stress-related chemicals like cortisol.

5. Scapegoats liberate other members of the family from duties
There's nearly always at least one family scapegoat in a dysfunctional household. They're used to shouldering the responsibility for all the family troubles. It offers a distraction from the problem itself and gives the family the compassion they want in social circles.. Financial mismanagement
Children who grew up in chaotic surroundings could never have learnt how to handle their money efficiently. Indeed, not having a positive example of paying

rent, and household costs can have a tremendous influence on them.

In addition, some dysfunctional families lack economic stability. Consequently, it's difficult for the youngsters to grasp the necessity of not spending everything they have on frivolous goods without thinking about tomorrow.

6. Learning violence
Have you ever heard that the abused becomes the abuser? Unfortunately, it's quite a regular event. It's because they never learned effective techniques of addressing conflict.

7. Self-medication with drugs and alcohol
Many individuals don't know how to deal with all the things that occurred to them in

the past, so they try to self-medicate to lessen the pain.

The problem with this mental process is that the numbness fades off as the drunkenness wears off, but they still have to confront reality.

8. Continuous suffering becomes bearable
Growing up among adults who constantly quarrel, or even avoid speaking, teaches youngsters that conflict is an inherent component of relationships.

While this is somewhat accurate since human disagreement is unavoidable, dysfunctional families teach unhealthy and insecure methods of dealing with conflict which becomes an issue.

If you're a parent or caregiver and fear you may be sliding into some of these dysfunctional family patterns, the least you can do is modify your actions.

To figure out how to deal with a dysfunctional family or how to heal from one, obtaining therapy as an adult may be the way ahead. By talking to a professional, you'll finally have the freedom to process your history in a secure, judgment-free setting.

Also, by doing it with someone who's trained, you'll discover it is possible to escape the cycle of neglect, abuse, or mayhem on your own. A mix of individual treatment and family therapy might be effective in breaking these unhealthy tendencies.

Chapter 4

Ways to cope with it

The first step is to take excellent care of yourself—"surround yourself with people who really make you feel good and uplifted. Their significant presence in your life will assist offset and buffer you from the negativity and other damaging conduct from a family member that has a poisonous influence on you.

The next stage is to seriously think about what you want for this relationship: Is it less touch, in general? Fewer phone conversations? Less digital contacts Consider what the connection might look like in this new form—"you can adjust your method of communicating in the future if things improve with little contact. Once you have envisioned this new connection, you may have a talk about the new parameters: Clearly describe how you want to connect in

          29

the future and practice what you want to say in case the discussion doesn't go the way you'd wanted.
Of course, it's also necessary to take precautions to shield oneself from the family member's poisonous conduct.

Here's how:

Recognize patterns and triggers of the person's toxicity so you may figure out how to attempt to dodge it, suggests Stoycheva.

Set boundaries on themes you are ready to discuss with the person and which ones are off-limits. Enforce them as time goes on.

Avoid conflicts with the individual. Remember that "the word no is a full sentence—you may just say no without elaborating or defending yourself,

Try to restrict your interaction with the individual in general and avoid engaging

     30

with the family member when you do see them.

Put the brakes on the person's destructive conduct. You may remark, This is not a conversation I want to have then leave the room or end the phone call.
It's crucial to reinforce and preserve your "conviction that you don't need to connect with someone who is mean-spirited and rude to you and hence toxic for you,
When the individual exceeds the limits you've set and/or behaves inappropriately toward you, be prepared to stick by your rules of engagement. There may be many occasions when you need to terminate the conversation, leave the table, or repeat yourself again and again about the value of courteous speech and following the limitations you've set,
So instead of asking him to her house for dinner, she offers to take him to watch a movie or eat out at a restaurant (where there's a natural time restriction) and brings

      31

her husband and kids when they're available (based on the belief that there's safety in numbers).

Family members represent a group unlike any other because we are linked to them. And that means it may be considerably difficult to cope with them simply because we assume we can't get rid of them. It's considerably more problematic when individuals are blood related, and when, since you are family, you will probably need to be near them on numerous occasions.

Up close and personal, toxic family members may include your parents, your siblings, aunts, uncles, grandparents, and anybody distantly connected to any of them. It's hard to cut somebody off when those close to you are still associated with them. It's hard to cut someone off when other family members have clear beliefs and attempt to weigh in. Being related complicates issues but the reality is, when all else fails, we can and often need to ban specific family members from our life.

Chapter 5

Dealing with them

Even if poisonous individuals came with a warning tattooed on their skin, they could still be impossible to avoid. We can always choose who we let near to us but it's not always so easy to wipe away the toxins from other portions of our lives. They could be coworkers, bosses, in-laws, step-someones, family, co-parents ... and the list goes on.

We live our lives in communities and unless we're ready to do it alone – work alone, live alone, be alone (which is occasionally enticing, but comes with its own consequences) – we're going to cross paths with others we would rather cross out.

With any discussion of toxic individuals, it's crucial to remember that you can't change someone, so it's better to quit trying. Save your energies for something easy, like global peace. Or landing on a star. The truth is that, when you do something differently, things can't help but change for you. If it's not the individuals on your radar, it will be their influence on you.

"Personal power is everything to do with what you believe – and nothing to do with what others think."

Co-existing with toxics is going around them to make your own rules, then realizing that you don't need them to obey those rules to claim your authority. Here are some great, practical methods to achieve that:

Be energized by your motives. Sometimes toxic individuals can trap you like a hunted object - you know you don't have to give in to them but you also know that there will be consequences if you don't. The idea is to make your decision from a position of authority, rather than feeling dominated. In the same manner there is something they want from you, there will always be something you desire from them (even if it is to escape more of their poison) (even if it is to avoid more of their toxicity). Decide that you're doing what you're doing to control them and their behaviors – not because you're a victim of their manipulation. Personal power is everything to do with what you believe and nothing to do with what they think.

Understand why they're seeing what they see in you.
Toxic individuals will constantly perceive in others what they don't want to admit about themselves. It's called projection. You may be the kindest, most giving, hardest working person on the earth and toxic individuals would turn themselves inside out trying to convince you that you're a liar, unjust, ugly

or lazy. See it for what it is. You know the truth, even if others never will.

They could become worse before they leave you alone.
Think about it like this. Take a small human who is throwing a tantrum. When you stay firm and don't give up, they'll go harder for a time. We all have a predisposition to do that — when whatever we're doing stops working, we'll do it more before we quit. Toxic individuals are no different. If they've discovered a technique to control and manipulate you and it stops working, they'll do more of whatever used to work before they back off and find themselves another victim. Don't interpret their escalation as a stop sign. Take that as a sign that what you're doing is teaching them that they're previous behaviors won't work anymore. Keep continuing and give them time to be convinced that you're not going around on the decision you've made to shut them down.

"Teaching Kids How To Set & Protect"
Be explicit about your boundaries.
You can't satisfy everyone, but toxic individuals will have you convinced that you can't please anyone - so you strive harder, work harder, sacrifice more. It's exhausting. Toxic individuals will have your boundary ripped down and buried before you ever remember you had one there. By understanding exactly what you'll accept and what you won't – and why – you can decide how far you're ready to let someone infringe on your limits before it's just not worth it any longer. Be ready to listen to that voice inside you that lets you know when things aren't right. It's strong and seldom wrong (if ever) (if ever). Whether someone else thinks it's correct or bad doesn't matter. What counts is whether it's correct or bad for you. Let that govern your reaction and when you can, who's in and who's out.

You don't have to aid them through every problem.
The reason why toxic individuals are often in crisis is because they are expert at generating them. It's what they do — draw breath and create drama. You'll be called on at any hint of a crisis for compassion, attention and support, but you don't have to run to their side. Teach them that you won't be a part of the pity party by being unemotional, inattentive, and apathetic to the problem. Don't ask inquiries and don't give aid. It could feel horrible since it's not your typical manner, but remember that you're not dealing with a normal person.

You don't need to explain.
No is a complete phrase and one of the most powerful words in any language. You don't need to explain, justify or make excuses. 'No' is the sentinel at your front gate that makes sure the pollution from hazardous individuals doesn't get through to you.

Don't judge.
Be understanding, caring, kind and respectful – but be all of those to yourself first. You may reject actions, requests and individuals without turning yourself into someone you wouldn't wish to be with. Strength and compassion may exist nicely together at the edge of your boundaries. It will be always simpler to feel comfortable about setting up a barrier if you haven't wounded someone else in the process. When it comes to letting go of connections with our toxic family members, we have certain alternatives accessible to us. I know from experience and through treating others that it is vital to attempt all of these possibilities. When we try everything, it makes our final decision to go no-contact more comfortable as we come to recognize the toxic individuals in our lives leaving us with no other alternative.

Set Clear Boundaries
It might be challenging to establish and set limits if you're from a household that doesn't honor or respect them. You get to determine what therapy you'll accept now, though. Martin advocates addressing your wants and feelings honestly. You could beg your family member to modify their conduct, such as stating, "Please don't cuss at me."

"This is not generally successful with toxic people because they're not driven to modify their behavior," she explains. Instead, the barrier helps remind you to defend yourself against their methods. For example, you could hang up the phone or block your sibling's number if they continue to cuss at you during a call.